CHINSTRAPS
NOSE-MOULDS
& CORSETS

CHINSTRAPS NOSE-MOULDS & CORSETS

A Shopper's Guide to Feminine Beauty 1800s—1930s

Rosemary Hawthorne

Michael O'Mara Books Limited

Dedicated to All Women Who Need Encouragement

Rosemary Hawthorne, a fashion historian and clergywife,
has written books on Knickers, Manners and Agony Aunts

First published in Great Britain in 1999 by
Michael O'Mara Books Limited
9 Lion Yard, Tremadoc Road
London SW4 7NQ

A CIP catalogue record for this book
is available from the British Library

ISBN 1-85479-444-2

1 3 5 7 9 10 8 6 4 2

Edited by Yvonne Deutch
Designed and typeset by Martin Bristow

Printed and bound in Singapore by Tien Wah Press

CONTENTS

INTRODUCTION

This is a book about things women have wanted or needed – to make them feel 'better'. Women have *always* wanted 'something' because they believed they would become lovelier, happier, nicer and therefore more pleasing and desirable.

'If only . . .

. . . I had a better figure, nicer skin, bigger eyes, smaller feet, prettier hands, smarter clothes, a newer house . . .' and so on. In their hearts women sympathise with Cinderella's sisters because, truth told, we've all had 'ugly' days – often *very* ugly days – brought on by a feeling of dissatisfaction. Although, outwardly, it's beauty products and clothes that *seem* to give women confidence and sense of self-worth, there are other, less obvious (indeed, well hidden!) items that women have thought highly of over the years.

Some of those are very basic and go unrecognised as female morale boosters. In whatever sense the word 'love' has meaning, most women like to believe they are *lovely*. Convincing them they can, with ease, become better, nicer, bigger, smaller, prettier, smarter and newer – has always been skilful work for purveyors of temporary vanities and transient wonders. For centuries, the seeds sown in advertising to beguile women have fallen on fertile soil. Women *want* to believe. The 'sell' has been soft – the trick being to create a feeling of promise. Then, as now, it

has been essential to make the product unforgettable, choice, outshining all others and, somehow, within reach.

This anthology of advertising with the female psyche in view passes through 120 years of vanity, frailty, desperation and delight – and, naturally, I have thoroughly enjoyed selecting each device for the temptation of Eve. The only device I do not attempt to advertise is a man!

Rosemary Hawthorne
Tetbury 1999

Mama Knows Best

Weymouth, May 20th 1824

Dearest Mamma,
I am in a state of delicious confusion. Aunt Augusta has received an invitation for us to dine with the Misses Whitshed on the fifth of June and attend the Ball given at Salisbury Old House by their Godmother, the Countess of Ilchester. Should I wear my red *gros de Naples*, bordered with puckered crape or the dove silk with satin trefoils and blue velvet mantle trimmed with

swansdown? I will get Parry to dress my hair in an Apollo knot with your pearl diadem. Please send, post haste, a box of Mr. Pears' unguents . . . my complexion ails from so many routs.

Your loving and dutiful daughter,
Cecilia

Chelsea,
May 27th 1824

Dear Child,
Excellent news! There is no confusion, Sweet
Heart. Wear your India muslin embroidered
with silver and be sure to don silk drawers.
Your blue mantle will look well enough. I
have today sent, by special carrier, a box
containing samples of Mr. Rowland's
excellent Cosmetics, recommended by many
ladies in Town and thought superior to other
preparations of this kind for enhancing a
jaded complexion.

    I have included a case of silvered pins
for your hair. See Parry rubs them up.
My felicitations to Aunt Augusta.

As always,
Your affectionate
Mother

An Alabaster Brow

96 Punk Lane,
Brixton

Dear Dr. Booth,
A friend in my profession (dance and mime
artiste) has told me of your stuff that can cure
freckles and all sorts of skin troubles. I have
some eruptions in a difficult place.

Please send me a bottle as quick as
possible.

I cannot make up the stamps but here is a
back stalls ticket to the Alhambra Theatre,
Clapham, where I am a *modele* in a *tableau
vivant* in the Second Half. 'Salome and Her
Maidens'. Miss Jenny Lind comes on after us.

I hope this suits.

Ever so truly yours,
Miss Tabitha Tate

*'Both these pictures are taken from photographs of
the Baroness — —, Berlin, Germany. She is 44,
and got rid of her wrinkles after using my treatment*

*for only 4 months. She is now one of the famous
beauties of the city . . .'*
*'A lady told me she would be willing to give me a
£1000 pounds to get rid of her wrinkles . . .'*
The advertiser was onto a winner, yes?

SCENE: *Street Trader in the Haymarket*
'Ere you are, ducks, straight from Gay Paree,
city of pretty wommin' – jus' wot you needs
ter keep yer skin lookin' as fresh as a baby's
botty ('though some of those don't smell like
new mown hay!). 'Ere I 'ave a big bottle o'
'ANTI-PHALLIC SKIN MILK' to wipe away
those cares an' woes, plus any old rust marks,
spots or pimples that stops your dear faces
lookin' like lilies at Easter. For sure your
hubbies won't know you when they wakes in
the mornin' – they'll think they've died and
gorn to 'eaven. No, I'm not askin' a greedy
French fortune fer this Ferment of Delight
. . . I'm not even asking five bobs . . . let alone

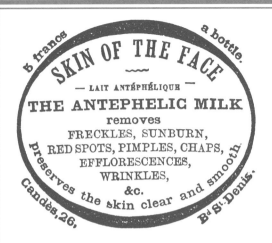

five francs! Ladies, Ma'mselles all, roll up, roll up. Take from my 'and this elixier of youth and replace it with *not* one florin piece but *one* 'ole shillin'. One shillin' for the banishment of a 'undred and one blemishes.

THE COURT HAIR DESTROYER.

3, Bottom Steps,
Lower Mills,
Bolton

Dear Sir,
My sister is in dire need of your 'Destroyer' for her face. Our Mam says she will lock her in a cupboard for she is ashamed to see our Annie walk abroad. I send the P.O. as asked.

I trust and pray the potion does effect a remedy for we fears she has no prospects to wed because of this affliction.

Yrs. faithfully,
(Mrs.) Hannah Pendle

Leading Ladies

It is interesting to observe that by the 1880s advertising recommendations for beauty products included well-known actresses or 'leading ladies' – as well as the time-honoured references from aristocratic Society women. Overt approval by the likes of royal favourites such as Mrs. Langtry was bound to improve the manufacturer's chance of finding a popular market. The other novel, but acceptable credential was that given by a doctor, especially a *lady* doctor.

Nothing changes!

For centuries beauty preparations had been made from natural ingredients, but by the 1880s a 'pure and healthy' angle was part of the sales pitch. In a market that was now

crammed with agents trying to market hundreds of different brands, with both natural and synthetic ingredients, these 'genuine' examples were projected as righteous products. Their makers cast themselves as agents of good, battling against 'spurious' rival brands which were being forced onto an innocent public by commercially minded villains.

Mmm! But . . . how very useful it was that Doctor Kingsford's family happened to own an established chain of Chemist shops?

Fresh as Dew

RIMMEL'S TOILET VINE-GAR is celebrated over the whole world for its useful and sanitary properties, and its delightful and refreshing Aroma. Price 1s., 2s. 6d., and 5s. RIMMEL'S LOVE'S MYRTLE and BRIDAL BOUQUET are the leading Perfumes this Season. RIMMEL'S TABLE FOUNTAINS, to play Plain or Scented Water, from 10s. 6d.

Sold by all Perfumers and Chemists; and by EUGENE RIMMEL, 96, STRAND, and 24 Cornhill, London; and CRYSTAL PALACE SYDENHAM.

By the turn of the nineteenth-century advertisers were most aware that middle and upper-class women sometimes travelled, long distances by train, boat and open motor-carriages – and often wished to have some means of 'freshening' up during these journeys. Mrs. Pomeroy, whose beauty

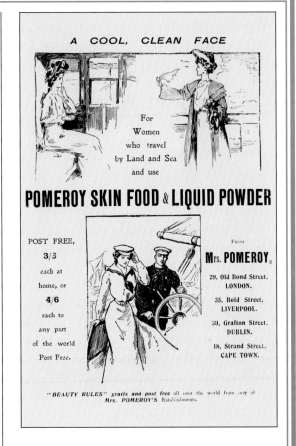

A COOL, CLEAN FACE

For Women who travel by Land and Sea and use

POMEROY SKIN FOOD & LIQUID POWDER

POST FREE,
3/3
each at home, or
4/6
each to any part of the world Post Free.

FROM
Mrs. POMEROY,
29, Old Bond Street, LONDON.
35, Bold Street, LIVERPOOL.
39, Grafton Street, DUBLIN.
18, Strand Street, CAPE TOWN.

"BEAUTY RULES" gratis and post free all over the world from any of Mrs. POMEROY'S Establishments.

emporiums set in London, Liverpool, Dublin and Cape Town would definitely find custom with wealthy, women sea-voyagers, would have sounded just the right note in her 'A Cool, Clean Face' copy line – for, as we know, there's nothing like a sea-breeze – and a sailor – to bring a flush to a lady's cheeks!

Eye Appeal

ARTIFICIAL EYEBROWS.

THE BEAU IDEAL of BEAUTY is well-defined eyebrows, the absence of them the greatest possible disfigurement. UNWIN and ALBERT supply artificially perfectly natural-looking eyebrows, 21s. the pair, forwarded on receipt of P.O.O. with colour desired.

For hundreds of years, women used *belladonna*, extracted from deadly nightshade to enlarge their pupils, giving languorous eye-appeal, and up to about 1870 a discreet amount of shading was seen in Society circles. Then the rules became stricter; 'ladies' distinguished themselves by *not* 'painting' – this was only for actresses or other 'low' women. A revival of eye make-up began in the early twentieth century and outlined eyes, darkened brows and lashes were once again seen on upper-crust faces, copying the new 'star' film actresses. But it was a reticent campaign – the first advertisements I found

YOU can have Beautiful Eyebrows and Long Lashes if you use EYEBROWLIN

THE SECRET OF SOCIETY LADIES' BEAUTY.

BEFORE AFTER

Why not follow the lead of Society Beauties and use this marvellous preparation? It does not stain, is perfectly harmless, and is recommended by leaders of fashion. A few applications of "EYEBROWLIN" will enable you to produce that dark, fascinating appearance admired by women.

Send 9d. in stamps to-day and receive a supply under plain cover.

Send at once to your grocers, JEAN BINET & Co. (Dept. A), 34, Strand, London, W.C.2.

for 'eyes' were in magazines of 1918 when an 'Eastern cum Egyptian' look was becoming all the rage.

But, who could resist the effect of a pair of false eyebrows in 1880? So 'natural' – and only 21 shillings the pair!

Long lashes fluttered everywhere; 'Laleek' – 'used by Royalty'– being a sort of coloured 'ointment' that helped lashes to sprout. For glamorous nights, lashes were swept up with brush-loads of sooty 'mascara' – a 'cake' requiring moistening (with spit!) to make it tacky but 'Tangee' made the first waterproof cream mascara in the 1930s.

LONG, LOVELY LASHES can be yours by simply applying Laleek "Longlash" — a *real* eyelash grower—specially created by Adelaide Grey, the Bond Street Beauty Specialist.

Obtainable in dainty, unbreakable container in 4 waterproof shades : Midnight Blue, Copper Beech, Raven Black and Colourless. Medically approved and used by Royalty. From all leading Stores, Chemists, Hairdressers, Boots, Timothy White's and Taylors, or direct from Adelaide Grey's salons. **Price** 1/- (Special brush 4d.)

LALEEK LONGLASH

Face Massage at my Salons, 3/6. Consultations Free. Phone: REGent 5825

ADELAIDE GREY 27 OLD BOND ST. LONDON. W.1

Powder and Paint

Elizabeth I had used cochineal and gum of Arabic to paint her lips and early 'lip-salves' were 'rouge paste' – often loaded with toxins. The first cased lip-stick was produced in 1895 but in the 1920s, against strong competition, 'Tangee' was to become 'The World's Most Famous Lipstick', supposedly ending that 'Painted Look'.

'Tangee' was brilliantly marketed; selling in Woolworth's, its 'colour changed by magic' when applied, becoming a 'natural' shade on the lips. In its slim, black Art Deco holder, 'Tangee' was unlike the tiny stumps of harsh carmine from before.

The other legendary lipstick

TANGEE

A thousand magic shades!

A thousand hues in one magic lipstick · Tangee! A lipstick colour which is yours and yours alone . . . . Which blends perfectly with your natural colouring, no matter what your complexion. Apply Tangee and the colour changes to the one individual shade you need!

Tangee is entirely unlike any other lip-stick. It contains no pigment. Magically it takes on colour after you apply it. It leaves no greasy smear. It is permanent. And because of its unique solidified cream base, it soothes and protects.

Whatever your colouring · Tangee is for you. One of its thousand shades is yours!

Tangee Lipstick, 4/6. The same marvellous colour principle in *Rouge Compact*, 3/6. *Creme Rouge*, 4/6. *Face Powder*, blended to match the natural skin tones, 4/6. *Night Cream*, both cleanses and nourishes, 4/6. *Day Cream*, protects the skin, 4/6. *Cosmetic*, a new "mascara," will not smart, 4/6.

SEND 1/- for TANGEE BEAUTY SET
(Six items in miniature and "The Art of Make-up")

CALMON & NEATE LTD., (Dept. 16).
8 Goynard Street, London, W.1.

from the 1930s is 'Tattoo'. How exotic, how powerful this beautifully presented advertisement is, even now. It is immediate, modern – its imagery reaches inside a woman's fantasy world. It connects with sultry tropics and being drop-dead, film-star gorgeous. Utterly wicked! You only need to buy this lipstick (a hefty four shillings and sixpence – serious

Tattoo your lips!

Wicked NEW shade!
"HAWAIIAN"
A brilliant, vivid brighter red

4/6
Refills: 3/6

"HAWAIIAN"—
a New Red from the South Seas

The *brightest* red ever! Daring, stunning, and positively indelible! TATTOO "HAWAIIAN"! And only TATTOO could give you this fetching *new* shade in an infinitely *indelible*, extremely *transparent* lipstick which positively will not turn the least bit purplish! Four other simply ravishing shades, too! . . . all giving exotic transparent stain instead of greasy coating. TATTOO is the South Sea maiden's secret of lovely lips. You simply put it on . . . let it set . . . wipe it off . . . only the colour stays! Behold, there are your lips . . . evenly, smoothly *stained* with transparent glowing colour . . . tattooed! Soft, inviting, youthful lips . . . luscious alluring colour that does not smear but stays on . . . through cocktails, cigarettes . . . *everything*! No dryness, no puckered lips, no pastiness. Fling a challenge to adventure . . . Tattoo your lips!

CORAL has an exciting orangish pink tint. Rather light. Ravishing on blondes and titian blondes.

EXOTIC is a truly exotic new shade, brilliant and transparent. Somehow we just cannot find the right words to describe it, but you'll find it very effective. It is our choice of them all.

At the TATTOO Colour selector on the better counters, connect yourself, you can actually test on your own skin all the TATTOO shades.

"HAWAIIAN" is the newest, reddest red yet. Brilliant, tremendously daring, this new shade has been dreamed of since lipsticks were first made. Positively won't turn purplish.

NATURAL is a medium shade. It is a true, rich blood colour that will be an asset to any brunette.

PASTEL is of the type that changes colour when applied to the lips. It gives an unusually transparent richness and a depth of warmth that is truly amazing.

TATTOO

DISTRIBUTORS: FASSETT & JOHNSON LTD., 85 CLERKENWELL ROAD, LONDON, E.C.1. TELEPHONE CLERKENWELL 2336

Green Face Powder

IN BOXES, SIFTERS AND COMPACTS

FOR a perfect complexion use Green Face Powder. Its pale apple-green shade gives the skin the fashionable ivory appearance and tones down any redness of face and nose.

For day and evening use the skin looks extremely natural.

1/6ᵈ

You can purchase this novel beauty aid, in sifter box **1/6**, gilt compact box, **2/6**, or in dressing-table box, as illustrated, at **3/-**. The Phyllis Earle Beauty Book is included free and your money will be refunded in full if dissatisfied.

vulgar for a girl to indulge in such a paper (although there were plenty of books written on the subject). There was still concern about 'regular' features, they had to be 'perfect' – so the combined Ear, Nose and Chin strap must had lots of customers. Hate your nose? Change it with a 'Trados' nose-shaper – and if it's still somewhat red and shiny, dust over with apple green face powder carried, well sifted, in a pretty compact.

money in 1936), coat your lips, and you are this creature of allure and temptation.

> I tried to kiss her lips so red
> Forever shall I rue it..
> 'Just kiss me it you dare!' she said,
> And I – I didn't do it.

But many a pair of 'Tattoo'-ed lips were kissed in the 1930s and 1940s.

The very fact that, by the 1930s, women could buy monthly magazines devoted entirely to 'Beauty' suggests how large the market for beauty aids had grown. In Victoria's day it would have been considered

The Doctor Recommends

A 'Dr.' here and a 'Prof.' there all helped to give beauty products discreet medical authority. In the nineteenth century, medical men and women were highly regarded by most of the population. They were seen as educated, caring, life-saving, professional gods who could be trusted. Although modern

ONE BOX OF DR. CAMP-BELL'S HARMLESS ARSENIC WAFERS will produce the most lovely complexion that the imagination could desire; clear, fresh, free from blotch, blemish, coarseness, redness, freckles, or pimples. Sent post free for 4s. 6d.—S. HARVEY, (Dept. 29), 12, Gaskarth Road, Balham Hill, London, S.W

Use DR. MACKENZIE'S ARSENICAL TOILET SOAP. Post free, 1s. 3d. per Tablet; three for 2s. 9d. Made from purest ingredients, and absolutely harmless.

generations would be alarmed – and rightly so – at the word 'arsenic' included in a list of ingredients for a beauty product – for hundreds of years this poison had been commonly used, albeit in small quantities, as a component for whitening the skin.

LOVELY COMPLEXION,

Skin clear as Alabaster, produced by one box of DR LENNOX'S HARMLESS ARSENIC WAFERS, the ONLY cure for Pimples, Blackheads, Sallow or Greasy Skins, no matter how bad. Price per enlarged box, sufficient for complete cure, privately packed, 5 6, post free. Absolutely harmless to the most delicate. Thousands of testimonials as to their marvellous effect.

REPORT by Dr Griffiths, Ph. D., F.R.S.E., London Nov. 11,1899: "I hereby certify that I have carefully examined and analysed Dr Lennox's Arsenic Complexion Wafers, which I find contain most valuable ingredients for beautifying the Skin and Complexion, and are quite harmless."

"ANALYTICAL REPORT by Granville H. Sharpe, F.C.S. "Dr Lennox's Arsenical Complexion Wafers contain in harmless combination a definite proportion of arsenic and other active bodies, and have a most favourable influence in preserving and improving the Complexion."

Dr LENNOX,

84, Bishopsgate-street Within, London, E.C.

Samples and Instructive Pamphlet post Free.

DR. MACKENZIE'S ARSENICAL TOILET SOAP.

Specially prepared as a beautifier of the skin and complexion, and guaranteed to contain a small but absolutely harmless amount of arsenic. Produces a lovely skin and complexion, and cures spots, pimples, redness, and freckles. The finest and purest soap made. For all irritations it is most emollient and soothing. Absolutely harmless. But beware of the many worthless imitations. Have Dr. Mackenzie's or none. At all Chemists and stores, **6d.** and **1s.** a tablet; 3 in box, **2'6**; or post free from S. HARVEY, London Bridge, S.E.

MADAME ADELINA PATTI writes from Craig-y-Nos Castle: "I find Dr. Mackenzie's Arsenical Toilet Soap most excellent."

MISS FLORENCE ST. JOHN writes from Oxford Street, W.: "I have been using Dr. Mackenzie's Arsenical Toilet Soap for some three months. It was recommended by a friend, and I was so pleased with the result that I have used no other. You are quite at liberty to publish my letter."

FRONT VIEW

SCENE: *A garden fence with two women talking over it*

'I see your Gert's got herself a young man, Mrs. Dyer? I keep see him walking up the path and then down with Gert on his arm. Is there a wedding in the offing?'

'Quite likely, Mrs. Bass. But not just yet.'

'Oh, why not? They look very moony whenever I catch them out the front window.'

'They are. But my brother's youngest, Sandra, is still having her treatment'.

'What treatment's that, then?'

'Her ears. Gert doesn't want a bridesmaid wearing a Claxton – even with flowers on it.'

Chin Up!

Out of all the hundreds of 'beauty ladies' who ran private 'establishments' at the turn of the century, the best was Mrs. Eleanor Adair. With salons in London, Paris and New York, snob appeal was her *forte*; her assistants were chosen with care – 'of gentle birth and sometimes daughters of medical men'. Her marketing was sensational, her advertisements riveting. Nothing fazed her. Sunk and doubled chins, ungainly flesh, superfluous hair, unwanted wrinkles, deflated muscles, tired eyes and shattered nerves. All were grist to her mill. A few weeks wearing the 'Ganesh Chin-strap' and you could look forward to being a new woman.

In *The Lady's Pictorial*, 1906, Mrs Adair charms and enlightens her readers in a lengthy discussion on the virtues of her treatments. To prove her point she supplies

samples of her many letters of support and admiration. As she says:

'Here are a few extracts from letters that show how thorough and useful the work of a true beauty-culturist is:'

"Dear Mrs. Adair, I think your 'Diable Tonic' is marvellous. My husband said after you had treated me that he had never seen me look so nice . . ."

"Mrs. Adair, Your 'Strapping Massage' has worked wonders for me . . ."

"Dear Mrs. Adair, All pretty women are clever women!"

"Dear Mrs. Adair, I have been doing your exercises and using the belt, and I look and feel better already."

What confidence! If anyone deserved the 1908 title 'Beauty Queen' it was the doughty, daring Mrs. Adair.

Take Away that Second CHIN

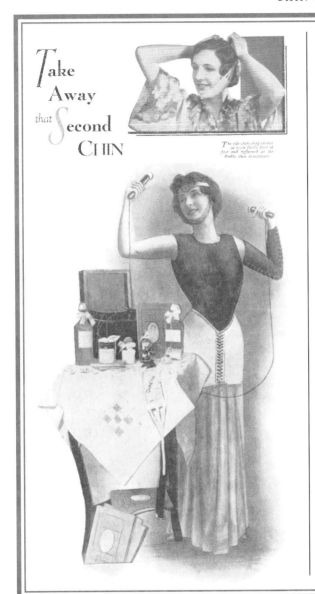

The silk chin strap should be worn fairly loose at first and tightened as the double chin disappears.

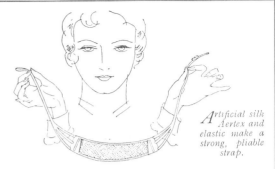

Artificial silk Aertex and elastic make a strong, pliable strap.

SCENE: *Lady demonstrating the wondrous 'chin-strap' at a Women's Institute Meeting:* 'Ladies, banish that double chin. A home-made chin-strap can be worn at night – or when you're certain there'll be no callers! This pattern's made from either *Aertex* or knitted. Mrs. Blundell has agreed to be my demonstrator model. Take the material, double it and bind the sides with pink sarcenet ribbon. Now sew elastic, like a hinge, to each end and have two longer pieces that button over the head – thus! It should be worn fairly loose at first and then *tightened up* by moving the button. Oops, *sorry*, Mrs. Blundell! I'll let them down again, now, dear.'

Bind the edges with pink or white sarcenet ribbon.

Sew on pieces of sateen on the slant, to allow for the bend of the chin.

A Beautiful Form

Women are never satisfied. One minute they want to be slim or even thinner – the next they want 'more' flesh – in particular, a full rounded bosom. Late nineteenth century American ladies must have had more than a head start with the invention of this trio of bosom friends. If you read the small print you'll notice that the nickel and aluminium 'Bust Developer' (which looks suspiciously like a sink plunger) will only work in harmony with, either a bottle of 'Bust Expander' or a jar of 'Bust Cream or Food'.

But to be sure of startling development you'd need to have bought the whole lot – and hope for the best.

This is one of my favourite advertisements.

It is full of uncertain promise.

Even fourteen years after the American Bust Developer there were possibly some women still eager to try for a challenge cup chest – risking heaven knows what in the process. If you read all the copy in the advertisement you will see that these desperate ladies might have been in danger of a runaway bust line, their bosoms daily increasing to proportions resembling pantomime pumpkins.

The price? Initially, at least, all this abundance for the price of a penny stamp!

It is amazing that anyone, however innocent, believed such extraordinary advertising like this, but faith can move mountains – or even help start build them.

A BLACK DAY when your bust begins to fall

EASY AS A BEAUTY TREATMENT. Moisten a pad of cottonwool with Kala-Busta milk. Apply gently. It is fragrant, soothing, gradually invigorating—then the miracle starts to happen!

SCENE: *Woman to mirror:*
'Oh, my God! Here it goes. My bust is falling. No – it's slipping and sliding – tumbling, even. It'll be round my knees soon. What can I do? I know, I'll try that treatment I saw advertised in *Woman's Weekly*. What was it? 'Kala-Busta', containing pure 'Naxolith'. 'Have you an unhappy sag that looks terrible?' Yes, yes, yes! Quick, how do I get some 'Kala-Busta'?

Send six shillings and sixpence; get bottle, one month's supply, by return. Now put 'Kala-Busta' on cotton wool, rub it on and wait for buoyant, beautiful, desirable breasts to appear.

Three months later . . . 'I'm still waiting.'

Delightful to Know

Victorian ladies often used depilatories
containing arsenical compounds while
Edwardian beauties glowed with *bouquet de
corsage*, but the barely-there evening dresses
of the 1920s and 1930s meant that even *more*
care was needed!

SCENE: *Mother on landing outside bathroom*
'Are you still in there, Phyllis? You've been
hours. Dance'll be all over if you don't hurry.
It's blunt? 'Course he 'asn't! Dad's got a
perfectly good razor of his own. No, I haven't
any idea why it's gone hard – perhaps you

MODERN WOMAN'S OWN RAZOR

The Duchess Safety Razor is specially designed for
ladies, and solves the problem of **UNWANTED HAIR**
once and for all.
This beautiful little razor has ONE DOUBLE CURVED
EDGE for underarm toilet and one straight edge for
neck and legs. It is indispensable to women who go in
for Tennis, Swimming or Dancing, and saves the risk of
powerful chemicals.
Razor Set Complete, 3/6, 5/9, 10/6 & 15/-.
Extra Blades, 2/6 for packet of five.

DUCHESS RAZOR

From chief stores and retailers or post free direct from:
DUCHESS RAZOR CO. (Dept. **W.5**)
318, Camberwell New Road, London, S.E.5.

WHY I USE NEW VEET

1 '*New Veet*' ends all unwanted hair in 3 minutes without trouble, mess or bother.

2 '*New Veet*' leaves the skin soft, smooth and white without trace of ugly stubble.

3 '*New Veet*' is just like a toilet cream — sweetly scented and pleasant to use.

4 '*New Veet*' avoids coarse re-growth—unlike the razor which only makes the hair grow faster and thicker.

FREE : By special arrangement with the manufacturers, every woman reader of this paper can now obtain a package of NEW VEET ABSOLUTELY FREE. Send 3d. in stamps to cover cost of postage, packing and other expenses. Address: Dæ Health Laboratories, Ltd., (Dept. **76 M**), Cunard Road, Acton, London, N.W.10.

didn't put the cap on the tube. When I was young, we used to cover ourselves up and wear gloves.

There's the doorbell; it'll be your Jack. I'll tell him to wait. Do hurry, Phyllis! So it hasn't got sleeves – whose fault's that? Deodorant? Put a spot of ammonia in the water, dab a lot of talc on. Oh – and remember not to raise your arms.'

Shining Tresses

An eighteenth-century 'shampoo' meant a 'lather' massage at a Turkish Bath. The Victorians had 'hair washes' made by soap manufacturers, but these could also be described as 'tonics', containing bay rum or quinine. Sears, Roebuck & Co Catalogue of 1897 advertised

'Shampoo Paste' to 'Remove dandruff, leave the hair soft and keep the skin healthy' and Sturrock's did a dry 'Home Shampoo' in 1900. 'Icilma' was a popular make and after 1910, wet or dry, they are commonplace. Firms like Evan Williams did a 1900s hot special; 'Paraphin Hairwash', but had more success with 'Tunisian Henna Shampoo' – 'red lights for mousy hair' and 'Chamomile'– 'for 'Blondes' in the 1920s.

> *Dan Druff*
> He sits upon my shoulder
> He scatters on my back
> I really think Dan's horrid
> And he hates me . . . in black!

Some products have catch phrases that secure them a place in history and are instantly recalled by millions of people.

Such a product was 'Amami' Shampoo – which came on to the market in 1926 already bearing the 'Friday night is Amami night' caption that made it famous. This was to remain a favourite shampoo for many years to come, the sachet that sent a girl to the 'flicks on Saturday afternoon with her sister and to the *palais de danse* in the evening with her man.

While they were riding high with success 'Amami' advertised many other beautifying aids – among them their manicure set. Victorian ladies prized pale hands (kept white with a rub of arsenical wafer or lemon juice) with neat, beeswaxed nails, buffed with chamois. Nail varnish, or 'polish' as it was polite to call it, was still a novelty in the 1920s and Good Society only thought well of the palest pinks. In 1930, Paris decreed that polish be applied to the pink part of the nail leaving the tips and half-moons *au naturel* – but Riviera beauties felt this looked anaemic with sun-tans (and diamonds), so blood red, vampire nails arrived. Meanwhile, 'nice girls' still played safe: thousands of handbags contained a tiny tin box containing a pink Amami 'Nail Polishing Stone' – 'Rub the stone on the moistened palm of the hand until enough adheres, then apply to the nails with light, rapid friction. A brilliant, pearly lustre is immediately imparted.'

As Nature Intended

Hair has always been a woman's crowning glory but to a Victorian woman, swathed in clothes from neck to ankle, it was probably the only visible, touchable, sexual attraction! Lovely hair won admiration from men, envy from women. Rich or poor, a woman who had the token luck to be born with beautiful (it was hoped, golden) hair had Mother Nature on her side . . . for the time at least.

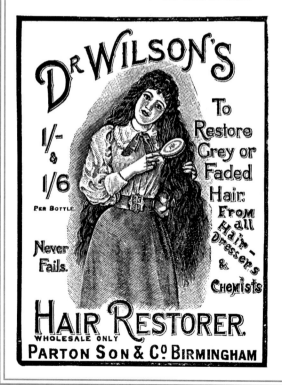

The 'growing grey' and 'hair loss' was a nightmare; everything had to be tried, including preparations by a sauce manu-facturer, to prevent this. We are still trying!

From *The Lady's Newspaper* 1849:

DR. LOCOCK'S Lotion for the Hair.—This highly-esteemed emollient Lotion, prepared from a recipe of the eminent physician whose name it bears, has proved most beneficial in restoring the hair, and when used daily, with the ordinary hair-brush, communicates a peculiar softness and brilliancy to the hair, and is alike favourable to its growth and permanency.

The continued use of this Lotion is generally sufficient for every purpose; but where the hair, from constitutional harshness, requires the occasional application of something more emollient, the MARROW POMADE, prepared by LEA and PERRINS, will be found to possess all those bland and nutritive qualities so peculiar to preparations of marrow, and which combine to render it the most suitable and agreeable Pomade for Nursery use.

Sold wholesale by the Proprietors, 6, Vere-street, Oxford-street; Sanger, Oxford-street; Barclay and Sons; Sutton and Co.; Edwards; Atkinsons; Prout, &c. &c.; and retail by the principal Chemists and Perfumers.

SCENE: *Delightful young couple, conversing . . .*

HE: 'Shall we go dancing tonight, Sue?'

SHE: 'That would be lovely, Colin.'

HE: 'What a pretty frock you've got on, Sue.'

SHE: 'I'm glad you like it, Colin.'

HE: 'You have such blue eyes, Sue.'

SHE: 'They are rather blue, Colin.'

HE: 'You have such a happy smile, Sue.'

SHE: 'I'm always laughing when I'm with you, Colin.'

HE: 'Your hair is simply lovely tonight – I feel terribly romantic . . . Sue.'

SHE: (*turning aside*) 'Thanks to "Camilatone Golden Rinse" – but that's *my* secret . . . Colin. (Oh dear! What a twerp!)'

Making Waves

Getting straight hair to curl, between 1890 to 1914, was down to rags, tongs or a Moore's 'Hot-Air Chamber'. Keeping it in place was up to a battery of ironware. Women had often used decorative combs and pins to lend charm and emphasis to hair-do's – but the actual fixing was done by an array of metal pins and snapping steel 'grips'. Kirby, Beard and Co. produced a 'pincer'-ended 'Security' hairpin in 1890 and forty years later had invented the famous 'Kirbigrip', but there were many other products that could deal effectively

with a set of waves, torrent of ringlets or toss of wayward locks.

The humble hairpin was one of the biggest manufacturing earners – ever.

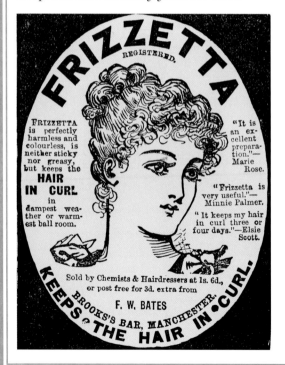

SCENE: *Pert young thing talking to her friend:*
'Oooh, like Anna Neagle? Well, people say so
... about the eyes. Her hair's like mine ...
now. My friend's a hairdresser and she's
comes round once a week and sets it. Mum
bought me some "Ladye Jayne's" to sleep in
from Selfridges. I've got two or three cotton
net ones for ordinary, a silk net one if I go to
stay with Cousin Mona and a beautiful lace
one for my honeymoon ... Ronnie, cheeky,
says he's glad I like *that* a lot because it'll be
the only thing I *will* be wearing!'

SCENE: *As a young hairdresser in Paris in 1870,
Monsieur Marcel Cateau, was 'crimping' his
mother's hair when the hot, double-pronged tongs
slipped in his hand – producing a continuous series
of waves on the lady's hair ...*
'Oh, Marcel, mon cher, vot 'ave you done?'
   'Ooh, Maman, I 'ave Marcelled myself!'
This happy accident created the famous

'Marcel Wave' and quickly made a fortune
for the entrepreneurial trichologist. The
technique was particularly successful on
shorter hair of the 1920s but 'Marcelling'
went out of fashion in the 1930s with the
American invention of 'permanent' wave
which 'fixed' the hair for several weeks.

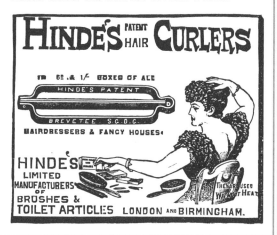

Added Attractions

By the late nineteenth century Society ladies piled their tresses, ideally 'golden', as high as humanly possible. Waved, banded and frizzed into great coiffures. As the silhouette grew taller, hats replaced bonnets, so a 'nest' of hair was vital on which to pin the *chapeau*. Wig-making, using real hair, was an art; young girls with keen eye-sight and nimble fingers were employed to make up the false 'pieces' – or 'transformations' – that were discreetly mingled with the wearer's own hair. Fringes and 'fronts' were popular; the 'Zephyr Cycling Fringe' was 'waterproof and curly'; the 'Butterfly' was for sea-side wear . . . but when was the 'Banshee' or 'Regent Dip' appropriate?

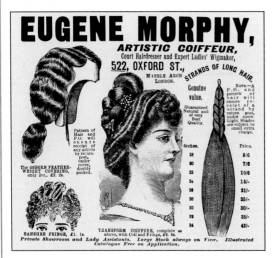

This little curl of glossy hair
She dropped it in the waltz,
I do not care to cherish long
Because you see . . . 'tis false.

Pearls of Wisdom

From *The World of Fashion* 1824:

MR. NICHOLLES, DENTIST, 15, Pall-Mall, DEVOTES his Professional attention entirely to affections of the Mouth, and the application of Artificial Teeth, under every circumstance of simple and complicated deficiency.—One to Six.

Nineteenth-century dentists were skilled and feared artisans. They also made a lot of money! Only the rich could afford these gruesome false teeth, said by a contemporary to 'look like the key-board of a spinet' – and the grim agony of tooth removal taken with . . . 'care and delicacy'. But the profession continued to gain a better, *slightly* less frightening reputation throughout the next hundred years. By 1912, advertisements for second-hand false teeth promised 'full value' to the seller!

"Have you cleaned your teeth?" began to take on meaning for the middle and upper

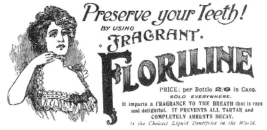

Preserve your Teeth!
BY USING
FRAGRANT FLORILINE

PRICE: per Bottle **2/6** in Case.
SOLD EVERYWHERE.
It imparts a FRAGRANCE TO THE BREATH that is rare and delightful. IT PREVENTS ALL TARTAR and COMPLETELY ARRESTS DECAY.
Is the Choicest Liquid Dentifrice in the World.

classes in the nineteenth century. For centuries, English nobility with decayed, rotten teeth were obliged to keep their mouths 'fixed' small when they spoke, to limit the offence of their breath. The Georgians sucked violet scented 'cashews' to sweeten the gusts, while Victorian actors were advised to take a swallow of 'breath scent' before a love scene. By 1850, people began to realise the virtue of brushing their teeth and numerous, new toothpastes, powders and 'soaps' began arrive behind chemists' counters. Alexander Rowland & Son's 'Odonto' lasted well – still being advertised and bought in the 1920s.

'My tooth-brush is a thing that haunts me when I'm travelling, and makes my life a misery' said Jerome K. Jerome in *Three Men in a Boat*.

But there was no need for dismay;

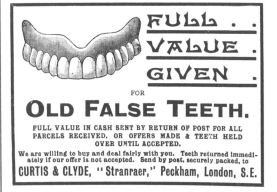

FULL . .
VALUE .
GIVEN .
FOR
OLD FALSE TEETH.

FULL VALUE IN CASH SENT BY RETURN OF POST FOR ALL PARCELS RECEIVED, OR OFFERS MADE & TEETH HELD OVER UNTIL ACCEPTED.

We are willing to buy and deal fairly with you. Teeth returned immediately if our offer is not accepted. Send by post, securely packed, to

CURTIS & CLYDE, "Stranraer," Peckham, London, S.E.

Rowland's Odonto
A teeth beautifier

PERSONAL LOVELINESS
Is greatly enhanced by a *fine set of teeth.* Don't lose sight of this fact, and remember to cleanse your teeth every morning with that supremely delightful and effectual dentifrice,
Rowland's Odonto
which whitens and preserves them without scratching or injuring the enamel; **2/9** per box. Sold by stores, chemists and at ROWLAND & SONS, 67, Hatton Garden, London.

O.S. TOOTH BLOCK.
MOST COMPACT FOR CYCLISTS.
BEST & SAFEST DENTIFRICE

healthy competition now abounded to save teeth from destruction. You could scrub away for all you were worth, trying out all these different brands of tooth-cleaner, while boating or even bicycling – and, Dr. Scott, who had already invented an 'electric' hairbrush, had an 'electric' toothbrush to go with it by 1885.

A Young Girl's Advice
My teeth are pearls, I hear you say,
Because I clean them twice a day
So even when I'm old and wained
My pearls will not be lost or stained.

The solid pink block of antiseptic-smelling tooth 'soap', with pleated, waxed wrapper fitting snugly inside a flat, round, silver tin

will be remembered by many. D. & W. Gibbs, who started as tallow chandlers and became 'sopers' in the eighteenth century, produced many beauty products, but they cornered the market with their 'Dentifrice'

(popular with troops in the First World War). They appealed to parents to safeguard their children's 'ivory castles'. Many a tooth fairy must have cause to thank them for a good haul of gleaming ivories.

Inner Cleanliness

The early Victorians never referred to constipation; it was indelicate. They spoke of 'cossitive bowels' and although there were numerous pills and potions – including the ever-ready castor oil – manufactured and swallowed by millions to relieve the situation, nothing has been so positively advertised for this condition as 'Beecham's Pills', 'Bile

Beans', 'Eno's Fruit Salt' – and Kellogg's 'All Bran'.

But the health-conscious 1930s had matters well in hand.

SCENE: *The golf course* 'Oops, dearie! Watch that swing! Guess what you've had for breakfast? Would we were all so free in our actions . . .'

They used to call her lazy!

She wasn't really lazy. She merely lacked strength and energy because she was so troubled with constipation.

She went to stay with friends—who made Kellogg's ALL-BRAN a part of their daily diet. And now she not only enjoys her breakfasts more (All-Bran and cold milk or cream makes such a delicious meal)—but she's free from the pill and drug habit; enjoys her golf; her tennis; her work.

But whether you need a gentle laxative or not you'll enjoy the delicious flavour of Kellogg's ALL-BRAN. It is 100% bran and supplies ample "bulk", Vitamin B and iron to build red blood. No cooking. Just buy a packet to-day—and eat two tablespoonfuls every morning.

FREE: "A New Way of Living," a complete booklet on constipation, also interesting diets, recipes and menus. Illustrated in full colour. Send a postcard for your free copy.

Kellogg's ALL-BRAN

KELLOGG CO. of GREAT BRITAIN, Ltd. Bush House London, W.C.2

Blessed Relief

Aargh! Trapped wind! What's more, in 1897, it is trapped behind a whalebone-fenced corset. No, not at all pleasant. Poor Mrs. Lawrence, the farmer's wife from Mid-Rasen, Lincolnshire must have had a grim a time of it – imagine being 'took bad' while crouched on a three-legged stool pulling at her cow's udders. This was before the soothing touch of Page Woodcock's Wind Pills arrived on the scene (how handy that he lived so near).

Oh, the relief it must have been to finally loosen the stay-lace and let it all 'go free'.

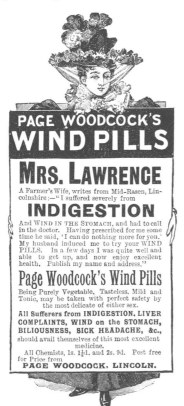

Cheat Your Mirror of Its Malice

In *Good Housekeeping*, 1922, the makers of Kruschen Salts told eager readers how to 'Cheat Your Mirror of Its Malice'

'. . . The morning light streams in upon your face; you lose heart. The truth is torn from you – you are "getting on".

You need toning up – all through.
Your digestion is all wrong.
You are sleeping none too well.
You get depressed for nothing.
Your nerves are all on edge.'

The lady says it tastes vile, but pop 'as much as you can get on a sixpence' in a cup of tea and you can't taste it.

I wonder – do they still sell it?

Supporting Role

Speaking of tummy pains – you'd have had real problems getting this appliance on – and off – in the twinkle of an eye. All those laces, big straps and buckles – especially on a cold morning. But what a wonderful result! A real shelf on which to sit that nine-month 'bump' – and afterwards a comfy seat to park those

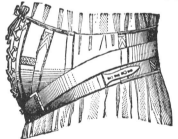

poor, stretched stomach muscles. Gran swore by hers; she hadn't taken it off since her twelfth, Sid, was born in 1861 – the year Prince Albert died. She said the comfort to her 'insides' was a blessing and worth being done up like a cabin trunk ready for Carter Paterson.

Chloroform cologne is another of those quasi-medical treats that Society women were able to indulge in. It is unlikely that working class girls had time for 'lassitude'. Queen Victoria had found chloroform vapour a great comfort during several accouchements thereby ensuring honour and respect for the Scottish physician, James Young Simpson. This 'cologne' is a charming, clever spin-off from the Doctor's great discovery. At the date this advertisement appeared Simpson had been dead for 31 years. Her Majesty, Queen Victoria had also died – in January 1901 – so *The Queen* magazine – and several advertisements – are bordered in funereal black.

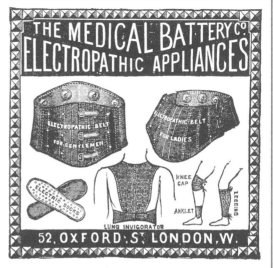

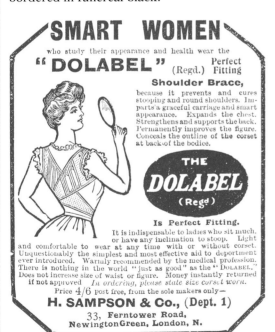

Electricity really sparked things off in the 1880s. Here's the 'Medical Battery Company' of 52, Oxford Street in 1886 being bang up-to-date and on-the-ball, providing ladies with some unusual 'warming' items of cure-all body wear. To fit the electricity bill, there are a few fantastic, original things designed by Mr. C. B. Harness, Consulting Medical Electrician to the above Company. C. B. H. suggests you try a lung invigorator, a tummy belt, leggings, knee caps – and, hang on, a brilliant idea this, electric socks! Now those would really make you jump!

And, of course, when the really smart lady needed a touch of bracing uplift, she had only to turn to the wonderful 'Dolabel' shoulder brace. Once strapped in, she was ready to face the world with perfect confidence!

Heightened Effects

SCENE: *Woman, in shoe shop, surrounded by shoes:*
'No, *not* bronze. In indigo? I'll *try* them in
French Calf . . . it's *so* difficult to clean.
Water-proof? They don't feel it and my feet
look big. I'm *really* a *small* five . . . well,
perhaps five and half in my left. A six? Well,
they pinch my toes and those slop about. I
wanted something I could wear in Town, but
I can't see anything. That heel's *so* high – and
the colour's *ghastly*. Why is it impossible to
find a nice, plain pair of shoes? I'm
exhausted; I'll just take the velvet slippers
with the flannel lining.'

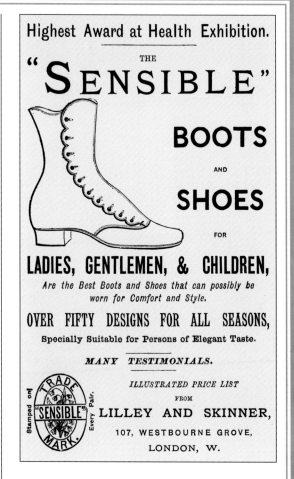

SCENE: *Suburban house in 1886.*
Mother showing daughter the advertisement.
'There you are, Gladys. A nice pair of *sensible*
boots from Lilley and Skinner's. They do up
at the side with that frilly edge – just like you

say you want . . . they're 'Specially suitable for persons of elegant taste' (hmm, fussy, I'd say) *and* they won the highest award at Health Exhibition. 'Over fifty designs for all seasons . . .'

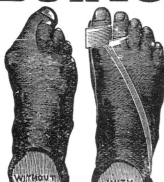
'I don't like them.'
'Why not?'
'Because they're sensible, healthy and *you* like them'.
'You girls are *ridiculous*! You wait. One day you'll have kids!'

Mousetrap Cottage, Titchfield

Dear Mr. Edison, I have seen your advertisement in *Woman's World* and hope that you may be able to help me.

Yours sincerely, O.I.M. Tiny (Miss)

A Weighty Problem

The late Victorians were aware of obesity and there were many products advertised to help you lose weight. For centuries, being fat went with the philosophy that 'you'd done well'; comfortable curves meant an ability to provide ample food. Beggars in the work-houses were skeletal. By the late nineteenth century, however, women's Society magazines, featuring photographs of fashionable beauties with 19-inch waists, increased a hundred-fold – young and slender now equalled romantic and successful. The cult of the slim had started. Young women did not want to look like a barrel of lard just to cherish their grandfather's theory that being stout put you in with the Top Ten Thousand.

Another advertisement offering a cure for obesity – this is one of a growing number

ALL FAT PEOPLE
Can be CURED by taking
Trilene Tablets
(Regd.)

For a few weeks. They will safely RE-DUCE WEIGHT and CURE CORPULENCY PERMANENTLY, whether Abdominal or General. They are small, agree-able, harmless, sent privately, and never fail to improve both Health and Figure without change of Diet.

AN ENGLISH COUNTESS writes:
" Your Trilene Tablets act admirably."

Send 2s. 6d. to Mr. F. Wells, The Trilene Company, 66, Finsbury Pavement, London, E.C.

THE ONLY CURE for STOUTNESS Registered by GOVERNMENT Price 2/6

to be found, not in Society magazines, but working-class 'Penny Weeklies' that were published in large quantities by 1918. Less well-off women now began to favour the 'slim' look and fashionable awareness increased further as the film industry gained

A 5/- Box of MY FAT CURE FREE
To Any Lady to Try.

I have set aside 5,000 5/- boxes of my remedy for free trial. Send your name and address to me to-day and accept one of these packages. My offer is open only to any lady who is subject to over-fatness, and who has not yet tried my remedy. If you are satisfied with the remedy pay me 5/-. If not, pay nothing. My remedy is for women only, and I can only send one package to each lady.

Mrs. M. SEYMOUR, (Dept. A.P. 6), Halsey House, Dane Street, London, W.C. 1.

Cinematic filming in the 1920s made actresses appear plump – especially with the shapeless, low-waisted dresses then worn. However, by 1930 Hollywood designers used bias cutting to create sexy, close fitting clothes that showed off – and lengthened the image of the female figure. Seeing this, more women craved a 'healthy' shape. There were lots of printed diets and pages of advice for slimming – in one magazine I counted twelve different advertisements for weight control. Some examples are: slimming tablets at one guinea a box; enrolling on a smart 'course' and learning 'how to'; or – definitely the easiest (and cheapest) – buy a packet of gum – and chew!

popular hold on public imagination. The advertisement below is an example of editorial copy being part of the subtle appeal – 'Beautiful Winifred Grace Hartland' is being 'interviewed' like a 'star' – but she happens to be the *product*; hence the printed (ADVT) at the end of the copy.

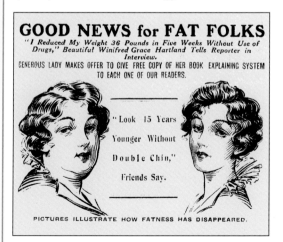

Bosom Friends

The bust continued to look up. After corsets covered by a camisole, various other designs of 'bust holders' emerged. First came the bust bodice: 'Creates a perfect shape by Centralising the Upper Portion of the Bust not Touched by Ordinary Corsets' (1902 advertisment.). Then, hard on its nipples, was the bust-supporter and later, the brassiere – which is, loosely translated,

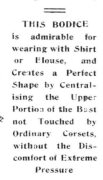

an 'infant's harness'. Curiously inaccurate, the French call a bra a *soutien gorge* – or 'throat support'.

The 1920 'Perfect' Bust Support blurb says it's invaluable to those engaged in 'active life'. How enjoyable.

The 'Arkella' took a combined approach:

Arkella
Guaranteed

SUSPENDER BRASSIERE.
This Brassiere gives a very attractive straight line effect, and entirely does away with that uncomfortable split between Corset and Brassiere. Suitable for all figures.
(Bust Measurement).
Model—Suspender Brassiere A, 2/6.
" " " B, 3/11.
" " " Satin, 4/6.

'This Brassiere gives a very attractive straight line effect, and entirely does away with that uncomfortable split between the Corset and Brassiere. Suitable for all figures.'

I bought myself a suspie-bra
Because I tried to please
My bust and waist and diaphragm
But not upset my knees.

Bust support was quite minimal in the sporty 1920s as the graceful Jantzen ad illustrates.

Wet One
Oh, beautiful limber Jantzen girl!
Arching your way to the summer-blue swirl
You fly by in your suit so sleek
Making all others look
Drab and not chic.

Oh, beautiful limber Jantzen sprite!
Have you ever felt swimming in ads.was trite?
How did you come to be such a belle?
Was it there in your genes
Or cast in a spell?

Oh, beautiful limber Jantzen maid!
In that red swimming cap you're sure to get laid!
I only advise to watch where you dive
They drained the pool water
This morning, at five.

Jantzen

JANTZEN Swimming Suits lend that smartness so essential in beach attire. The beauty of a swimming suit lies largely in its FIT, not only the way it fits before it is wet, but the way it stays fitted after it has been thoroughly wet and worn.
The gay colours, the advanced modes, the sleek well-fitting of Jantzen suits, are the real reasons for their leadership wherever swimmers gather. You can get Jantzen's at all the best shops . . .

Undercover Story

Fashion writer of 1900:
'Late October, a nip in the air and we are thinking about the fireside and toasted muffins for tea. For those of us who spend time in the country it's particularly important

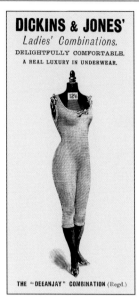

DICKINS & JONES'
Ladies' Combinations.
DELIGHTFULLY COMFORTABLE.
A REAL LUXURY IN UNDERWEAR.

THE "DEEANJAY" COMBINATION (Regd.)

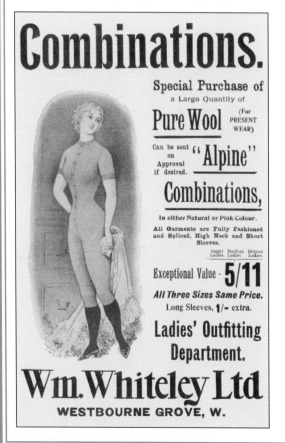

Combinations.

Special Purchase of
a Large Quantity of

Pure Wool (For PRESENT WEAR)

Can be sent on Approval if desired. **"Alpine"**

Combinations,

In either Natural or Pink Colour.

All Garments are Fully Fashioned and Spliced, High Neck and Short Sleeves.

Small Medium Outsize
Ladies. Ladies. Ladies.

Exceptional Value - **5/11**

All Three Sizes Same Price.
Long Sleeves, **1/-** extra.

Ladies' Outfitting Department.

Wm.Whiteley Ltd
WESTBOURNE GROVE, W.

to have that warm-as-crumpet feel underneath that is always such a joy in church. As the hunting season "drawers on", girls who are keen in the saddle realise the importance of having safe-guarded their seats by putting on some extra-specially secure combinations when mounted. In Town you will find lots of these in stock – many types, with fully fashioned, spliced bottoms in natural and pink, are sent on approval.'

SCENE: *Couple in their Victorian bedroom*
Him: 'Maude, what is it?'
Her: 'It's new.'
Him: 'I don't care. You're not wearing that in bed. You look like a sheep.'

Her: 'Mother bought it for me.'
Him: 'I thought I recognised her. Take it off. It's horrible.'
Her: 'It's my body – I can wear what I like. It's a llama sleeping vest.'
Him: 'Then give it back to the llama.'
Her: 'Mother said it would give me a restful night.'

Him: 'Then give it to her and they can take turns.'
Her: 'I won't take it off, I won't, I won't . . .'
Him: 'Then – go in the garden, Maude!'

D. H. EVANS & Co. LTD.

HOSIERY SPECIALITY.
WHITE
Llama Wool Sleeping Vest.

When ordering please send this illustration.
The lightest, warmest, and most comfortable Sleeping Garment ever produced.
Price **1/6½** Postage 1½d. extra.

Oxford St, London, W.

ART SILK KNICKERS

42 COUPONS

42 Bournville Cocoa coupons bring you a pair of fashionable art silk knickers with basque front. The colours available are ivory, sky-blue, pink, apple, maize, and peach. Why not get an art silk slip to match for 64 coupons? Send a postcard (postage 1d.) to "New Gifts," Cadbury, Bournville, for the complete list of over 200 Gifts, including Art Silk Vests, Stockings, Jumpers, etc., etc.

SCENE: *Young girl reading to her grandmother:* 'Forty-two Bournville Cocoa coupons bring you a pair of fashionable art silk knickers with basque front. The colours are – ivory, sky-blue, pink, apple, maize and peach . . .'

'Gran, look, that's a good offer isn't it? Forty-two cocoa coupons. Would you like a pair? Elastic top and bottom's in art silk – that's smooth and silky. What do you fancy? Apple, maize? How about peach? Peach would be nice?'

'I'd like the peach but I don't want to drink all that dratted cocoa!'

Simply Gripping!

For centuries stockings were held up (or not!) by garters. The late Victorians began to attach two front suspenders to the corset, but 'sussies' were still a novelty in the early 1900s and corset advertising, never backward in coming forward, was even more engaging . . . in every sense.

SCENE: *Dad looking at 1903 magazine:* 'I can see it's our Gloria. What's she doing prancing about in just her shimmy and a corset? Did you know about this, Mother? I think it's disgusting!

I'm going to write to Mr. Dickins and Mr. Jones. They should be ashamed to be named alongside near naked girls on page 3.'

By the 1900s, keeping stockings hoisted reached a new high; commercially speaking, the hooks were out!

In 1899 I. B. Kleinert Rubber Co – who, to underwear is what Brooke Bond is to tea – patented the 'Hookon' tab-fronted, double suspender holder. This had a quartette of dingle-dangles that could 'hook on' the front of an old, pre-suspended corset. But, in 1920, Mrs. Flora Spiers, Bless her, advertised her belt and braces contraption. The 'Hosegard'

"THE SPECIALITÉ CORSET"

DICKINS & JONES Ltd.
REGENT STREET, LONDON, W.

lessened strain on stocking tops as the 'sussies' were clipped to an inter-connected duo of frilly garters – coloured pink, sky-blue, and black or white. Americans still call suspenders, 'garter belts'.

Working Girl

There was once a blissful time when most comfortably-off middle-class households routinely employed domestic help. However, some less fortunate 'economy-ridden little housewives' had to do their own housework.

I wonder if these particularly hard-up readers of *Woman's Magazine* in 1929 were captivated by this breathless fashion write-up. It extols the latest thing in work-wear – Amazon Overalls – designed in Paris, no less!

THE LATEST PARIS-DESIGNED OVERALLS

Springtime. And all feminine thoughts are turned towards Paris fashions. Imagination lingers on these creations with all their glamorous appeal. Luxury. Extravagance. "If only I could afford . . ." is the beginning and end of all the daydreaming. You can! You can afford to buy Amazon Paris-designed Overalls. Overalls inexpensive enough for the most economy-ridden little house-wife—but oh! so beautiful!

AMAZON OVERALLS

A Sense of Occasion

Around 1898, Society Brides may have patronised 'Madame Sykes' Court Dressmaker. 24 Hanover Sq. They could choose from a variety of styles, including: 'The Lady Agnes Townshend Wedding, Bridesmaids & Travelling Gowns.'

SCENE: *Two Society ladies in conversation:*
'All that Bruxelles' lace, duchesse satin and kashmir. . . tell me, Clarissa, is Sykes frightfully expensive?'
    'No, not at all, Rosamund, just throw her a handful of titles and she'll probably do it for nothing.'

THE LADY AGNES TOWNSHEND'S WEDDING, BRIDESMAIDS' & TRAVELLING GOWNS.

THE BRIDAL,
BRIDESMAIDS'
AND
TRAVELLING GOWNS
OF
LADY AGNES
TOWNSHEND,
SISTER
OF THE PRESENT
MARQUIS
AND NIECE OF
THE DUKE OF FIFE
AND
LORD ST. LEVAN.

The above, WITH THE REMAINDER OF THE TROUSSEAU GOWNS, WERE DESIGNED AND MADE BY
Madame SYKES, 24, HANOVER SQUARE, W.

Mourning Becomes Her

In 1900 being correctly dressed for a funeral was important and shops were dedicated to supplying 'symbols of regret'. These needed careful selection, especially if you were a young widow – left in 'fortunate' circumstances.

SCENE: *Young widow with shop assistant:*
'It's on Monday. No, not cheap bombazette. Jack wouldn't want me to go third class. Yes, fully craped, Whitby jet cross and earrings, black kid gloves and one of those dear little bonnets with Parma violets on the side. Black taffeta ruffles under the skirt – Jack would like that. I'm looking forward to wearing it all. Oh, and I'll take a dozen 2-inch black-bordered hankies. People will notice when I cry at the funeral.'

Rags to Riches

Personal Column *The Ilkley Advertiser*, 1848: 'Cast-offs: heavy-weight robe of brown wool, trimmed with braid. Ideal for moors. Other dresses similar. Lots of black. Carefully home-sewn. Nothing fancy. Suit governess or clergy household. Owner selling due to purchase of new finery for book-signings.'

Apply: Brontë (Miss),
The Parsonage, Haworth.

Divided we Fall

Report from the Cycling Club for Ladies,
Drill Hall, Berkeley Square.
'We await the start of this year's 'Musical Ride' competition. Pianist and *pedallistes* are ready. Here's Mrs. Theodore Williams on her steel steed. Mounted in the normal manner she is skilfully propelling her bicycle backwards! The crowd cheers. Next, Miss Wetenhall, last year's winner, deftly manoeuvering two machines by just a foot action, now bends to pick up a third. A tense moment. Can she manage it?

What's that ripping sound? The crowd roars. Miss W's divided skirt has come adrift and left this brave contestant, in some distress – free-wheeling to 'Pomp and Circumstance' in her drawers'.

THE "HART" PATENT WORLD-FAMED CYCLING SKIRTS,

To prevent your Hat from Rising

USE

The "WINDWARD" HAT GUARD

Fix one clip each side of hat, push slide under the chin, and the "Windward" will do the rest.

If unable to obtain, apply to the makers, the A.R.G. Company, 7, Ely Place, London, E.C.

Indispensable on **Windy Days** when Walking, Cycling, Motoring, on Tram, on Bus, on Boat, on Pier. Is instantly adjusted and removed.

1/- each.

SOLD BY ALL LEADING DRAPERS.

Hat Trick!

Fix one clip each side of hat, push slide under the chin, and the 'Windward' will do the rest.

I wear my hat on windy days
I fix it with a guard
Although my hat stays on okay
My chin has gone all hard.

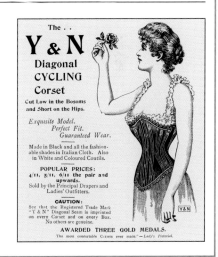

Scents and Sensibilities

SCENE: *Woman showing her friend her new bath:* 'Harriet, it's heaven! I can sit and wallow in warm, scented luxury for hours – well, until my skin goes rubbery. *Me* bought it for *me* for Christmas and spent nearly all Boxing Day in it (rather appropriate, don't you think?). While everyone else rushed off to be hearty and ride, walk, motor or play games in the beastly cold – I sat in my Cabinet reading a . . . you know . . .

naughty novel! This is the best 35 shillings' worth in Bond Street.'

Smart perfume – 'scent' is the 'U' word according to Nancy Mitford – comes in smart bottles, with a smart name. But a smell that is sought and remembered by *just* a number (remember, it's 'Chanel No. 5'), has to have been wisely advertised. Another classic, '4711' Eau de Cologne is a truly antique scent – (I bet there's still a bottle knocking around in Grandma's dressing table . . .) whereas the equally old 'Essence of Rhine Violets', beloved by Victorians, has sunk without trace. Perfumes go out of fashion but '4711' (Mulhens' batch number for this cologne perhaps?) lasted because it has always been in the 'refreshing' category . . . like a cold shower.

Moments of Reverie

Women always wish they could play the piano . . . beautifully. In our dreams, it is a summer evening and we're at the piano in a window overlooking the (perfect) garden – idly letting our (elegant) fingers drift over the keyboard, producing the most sensationally romantic bit of Chopin or Rachmaninov as effortlessly as breathing.

Why, oh why didn't we stick at going to Miss Hobbs' for lessons after tea on Friday's?

𝒯ℎℯ
AUTOPHONOLA
THE SUPER PLAYER PIANO

MAYFAIR STUDIO Upright Model 'A'

This 'Autophonola' *might* have been the answer. It contained a major advance for pretenders – the famous 'Flexible Striking Finger'.

The similarity of the 'Flexible Finger' to the human hand is . . . striking, don't you think?.

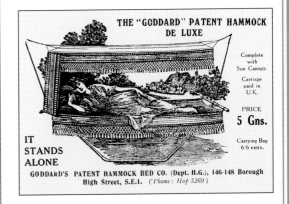

THE "GODDARD" PATENT HAMMOCK DE LUXE

Complete with Sun Canopy.

Carriage paid in U.K.

PRICE
5 Gns.

Carrying Bag 6.6 extra.

IT STANDS ALONE

GODDARD'S PATENT HAMMOCK BED CO. (Dept. H.G.), 146-148 Borough High Street, S.E.I. ('Phone: Hop 5269.)

Another thing women imagine themselves doing is lying in a hammock , looking ravishing. Not a nasty old, string contraption slung up somewhere near the coal shed but a gracious, heavily fringed, deeply cushioned affair with a canopy – the sort of hammock in which Cleopatra might have reclined while entertaining Antony.

The 'Goddard' Patent Hammock De Luxe *is* such a vehicle. Five guineas could buy you this wonderful dream-machine.

'It Stands Alone' reads the advertisement. You could say that!

Perfect Accessories

In the end, whatever they look like, whatever their mood – women want to be loved. You can try a bunch of roses, but nothing ranks alongside a diamond as the *true* outward and visible sign of that intangible emotion. Women have always adored diamonds; since the 16th century they've been going strong as a symbol of desire. They twinkle, they shine – and make a lady appear to do the same, beautifully. *Great* if you have a man to buy them for you! But, maybe, girls, you have to love yourself . . . and buy your own?

Diamonds aren't proud. They don't mind *who* pays.

Necessary for the well-being of a rich Victorian woman, while journeying, was her travelling case. This was a heavyweight article, a true 'hand-bag,' containing the items she might, perchance, find a desperate need to use *en route*. The costliest cases were silk lined, covered in water-repellent crocodile and filled with cut-glass bottles for lotions, potions – and medicinal brandy – as well as silver-mounted mirror, rouge and powder pots, brushes, glove-stretchers, shoe horn, scissors . . . and a clock. Mappin and Webb were one of many fine cutlers and luggage makers in London at the turn of the century.

Home Sweet Home

In 1900 you could buy a cottage . . . flat-packed. Get your plot, fix the foundations . . . whoosh . . . up . . . job done! Another 'want' satisfied. A 'roses round the door' number with two bedrooms, parlour, kitchen, scullery and indoor loo – all yours for seventy eight pounds, cash.

Cooper's promised to provide anything, from a pig-pen to a church, complete with portable, pitch-pine pulpit. So handy for itinerant vicars.

SCENE: *Woman standing with her husband by a new stove and reading the leaflet:*
'There's a delightful sense of freedom from back-bending and face-scorching to the happy owner of a "Valor-Perfection" Oil Cooking Stove. . .'

'Rubbish. You say your Mother said I'd like one for my birthday? Honestly!'

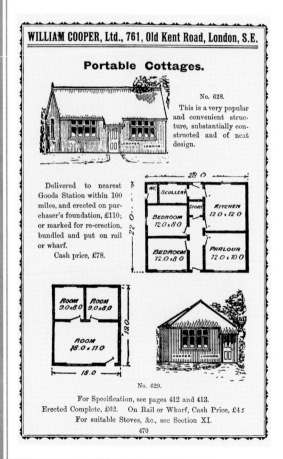

Baby's Carriage

The new baby's pram is an important accessory for a mother. To be seen pushing an attractive pram can much improve your

poise rating in the neighbourhood, even if the child inside is vile-featured. The Victorians had some beauties (prams *and* babies); they prided themselves on presenting an infant, layered in *broderie Anglaise*, in a carriage fit for a king, queen, prince – or any little frog that might pop up. Great Portland Street was the 'in' area for pram builders and the 'San Toy' (Telegraphic address: 'Todling, London') is a fantasy of curlicue cane on vast wheels. Just right for a little 'basket'!

The "ALBERTA" Baby Carriage.

Secret Blessings

A 'hush, hush' item created for women that's *really* made them feel a lot better – and with an interesting history? Sanitary towels, of course. In earlier days, rich women used hemmed diaper (diamond patterned) cloth; as for the poor, they had to use rags. It all meant tons of washing. The first disposable (actually burnable) towels were manufactured by Southall's in 1880. Soon afterward, Hartmann's, a German company, advertised their towels. Discreet ads. were placed in posh magazines – sanitary towels were costly and manufacturer's aimed their products at 'women who travelled' (your maid needing only a handy fire).

Fortunes have been made out of sanitary towels . . . but they took a 100 years to earn their 'wings'!

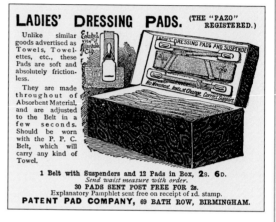

SCENE: *Matron speaking to girls at school:* 'Girls, I know it's hot and I'm sure you're all longing to swim but I want to show how you can protect yourself against embarrassment during 'the monthlies'. No, we don't call it

'The Curse', Thelma; sometimes it can be a blessing. This French Knicker has a special, loose 'hammock' part – (No, it's *not* mackintosh, Joan). Under a pretty party frock you may prefer this *Directoire* design – it's in such a discreet 'flesh' tone. Now, *this* pair would be ideal for games – it's got a lot of 'give' – *and* has a checked voile top. Wear it with the "Phantom" belt – or, excuse my fun, girls, you may want to jump over "The Moon"!'

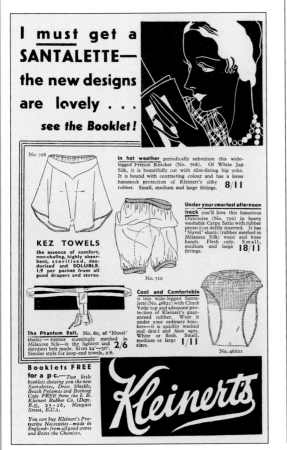

Perfectly clear

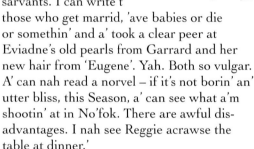

SCENE: *Aristocratic lady in her country house with eye-glass:*
'But, m'dear, they're an absolute boon! Yah. A' can nah see t'other side of the 'drawin'-rum an' see those tir'some, borin' things, like tha sarvants. I can write t' those who get marrid, 'ave babies or die or somethin' and a' took a clear peer at Eviadne's old pearls from Garrard and her new hair from 'Eugene'. Yah. Both so vulgar. A' can nah read a norvel – if it's not borin' an' utter bliss, this Season, a' can see what a'm shootin' at in No'fok. There are awful disadvantages. I nah see Reggie acrawse the table at dinner.'

When all else fails . . .

SCENE: *Woman alone with barman:*
'I'll just have one more *tinsy whinsy* one . . . Whoops! . . . Pardon me! I musn't get *tiddly* . . . must I? (*Hic*) . . . I don't care *that* much (*snaps fingers*) if he's left me for some little trollop! (*Hic*) . . . What do *I* care, right? I can get along fine without him . . . (*Hic*) . . . Pardon me!'
She leans across bar:

'It's all my own money, y' know? Every damn penny! Daddy left it *all* to me! (*Hic*) *Daddy! Dear Daddy!* (*cries*). He wouldn't have let the beast get away with it . . .'
'I'll just have one more *tinsy* drop.'
'And one for yourself, darling! (*Hic*).'